Funny Short Stories

Stories

Real Estate Agents
Share Their
Funny Short Stories
Volume 1

Edwin Almeida and Sue Elliott
FunnyShortStoriesBy.com

Disclaimer:

This book is intended for light reading only, the stories are actual events that were experienced throughout the authors careers as Real Estate Agents.

Fiction names have been used to protect the innocent.

Enjoy reading.

Funny Short Stories

Real Estate Agents Share Their

Funny Short Stories

Volume 1

FunnyShortStoriesBy.com

Acknowledgments:

My gratitude and thanks to my coaches and mentors:

Daniel Hall – the first person to awaken my interest in writing with his fabulous course "Real Fast Books".

Jay Boyer and John S. Rhodes whose step by step instructions in "Tablet Cash Machine" completed the big picture.

Finally my first of many books to come.

Thank you for being great teachers.

~~~~~~~~~~~~~

To my co-author and friend Edwin Almeida.

We have been through some challenging, soul searching and interesting times together.

During our brain storming sessions we come up with some weird ideas. This book is the first completed book project from these sessions. We have many to follow.

Enjoy your reading

Sue Elliott,
Sydney, Australia

Dedication:

Real Estate for the majority of home owners or investors is the biggest investment and dollar outlay they will experience in their lives.

Therefore high levels of emotion are often involved.

This book is dedicated to:

The hardworking Real Estate Agents in both Sales and Property Management who take their roles in this exciting process seriously.

Diplomacy is very important because of the often high level of money, emotions and personalities involved with two parties and their professional teams.

We, the Agents, need to wear many hats – a mediator, a negotiator, a networker, a therapist – at the same time knowing and abiding by all the rules and regulations associated with our industry.

The Licensees (Business Owners) who carry a large responsibility and sometimes burden, both emotionally and financially.

The individual sellers and buyers who take the BIG step into Real Estate.

Finally to the tenants, vendors and landlords whose stories we have shared in this book. Without these stories there would not be a book.

We hope the experience of Real Estate is rewarding and enjoyable to each of you.

Table of Contents

The "X – Rated" Section

Section 2: Bodies Exposed

Pages 59 – 80

Section 3 : A Tale About Landlords And Owners

Pages 81 - 100

Section 4 : The Essential Love Story

Pages 101 - 127

FunnyShortStoriesBy.com

Introduction:

The intention of this book is for some light relief and fun from everyday life in these times of global uncertainty.

Unless you're homeless every reader will hold at least one of these honorable titles of:

- Tenant
- Landlord or
- Home Owner

it is quite likely this book will have a story that you can relate to.

This book may bring a smile to your face, hopefully even a good laugh. Have you recalling some of your own funny experiences (if so we'd love to hear them).

Just as "JAWS" made most people think twice about swimming in the ocean. This book may make you think twice before you:

- open a cupboard or bedroom door (*Ripped Shirt And Band-Aids or Property Sold And A Divorce*)
- drink a cup of coffee (*Ben's Friends Share A Cuppa*)

- hang out your clothes *(Cat Habits)*

- step backwards without looking *(Dogs Habits)*

- open a door without knocking *(Gorgeous Blonde Surprised)*

- enter a bedroom unannounced *(A Perfect Open)*

Each Funny Short Story can be read whilst waiting:

- at the Vet's *(Super-Dog)*

- for an appointment with The Exterminator or a Tribunal hearing *(Ben* or *Creatures That Cause Depression)*

- for your Latte *(Pirates And Lesbians)*

- at The Therapist *(The Nigerian Money Scam)*

This leaves "*Men Can Look Sexy In An Apron*", "*She Treats Me Like A God – Burnt Offerings*" and "*Time Warp*" that are included 'just for the heck of it'.

Don't miss the conclusion - The Essential Love Story of "*Fred And Ginger*" - AAHH.

In this book you will **NOT** learn any:

- investment or property strategies
- ways to save tax
- ideas of working smarter (or maybe ....)
- marketing ideas ...... unless you acquire our Australian version of this book, that our Real Estate Agency uses as a marketing tool.

The Australian version of this book is called **"Untold Stories by ...."** as it's a series of books for various types of businesses, with Real Estate being the first.

"Untold Stories by Real Estate Agents" in addition to the hilarious (ok slightly funny) stories the book promotes complimentary and aligned businesses with strategically placed promotional advertising and marketing at a very affordable price.

A book is generally seen as an item of value which is kept (unlike a magazine or newspaper) and read, especially when the stories are funny and short.

A book is also a very unique marketing tool. Our office presents books as gifts to attendees of our Open Homes, to our buyers, sellers and Landlords.

The team members of
Just Think Real Estate

attend numerous networking events. The books are always popular and has created new business for our office that we would unlikely have achieved without them.

The promoters in our Australian books also use the books as marketing tools for the same reason, unique advertising and promotion.

For more information about:

"Untold Stories by Real Estate Agents" and how we market and promote the book in Australia through Edwin Almeida's Real Estate Agency, contact :

Just Think Real Estate

Suite 1,   4 Charles Street,   Parramatta,

Sydney,   Australia   **612 9635 6277**

Websites:
www.FunnyShortStoriesBy.com
www.Just-Think.com.au

You Tube Channel:
www.youtube.com/JustThinkProperty

Facebook:
www.facebook.com/Just.Think.Group

Linked In: Profile:
http://www.linkedin.com/profile/edit?
trk=hb_tab_pro_top

Linked In: Group:
http://www.linkedin.com/groups/Just-Think-Property-
4288955?gid=4288955&trk=hb_side_g

Twitter:
www.twitter.com/justthink1

emails: edwin@just-think.com.au

sue@just-think.com.au

sue@FunnyShortStoriesBy.com

submit your story online at:

http://untold-stories-by.tumblr.com

Section 1

Animal Behavior.

Section 1: Animal Behavior.

Chapter 1

Ripped Shirt
And Band-Aids.

Our agency runs a large rental department. Every rental property has a regular midterm inspection.

We invite our owners to attend the inspections with us so they can see first hand the effort we go to ensuring their property is well maintained. This also allows us to discuss any repairs that should be carried out and other relevant matters.

A midterm was booked for a unit. The tenants were two young women in their twenties who I affectionately refer to as 'the girls'.

On this occasion the owner was not attending, so I decided to show up a few minutes early.

As I knock on the door I hear people running, shutting doors and the typical sounds of panic associated with a midterm inspection when something is amiss.

Finally the door opens and I'm asked in. I chatted with the girls for a while, they seemed nervous, edgy, even a bit guilty.

From past experience this generally means one of two things. They have another person living in the unit or they've broken or damaged something.

I commenced my inspection of the unit, paying particular attention of signs of a third person living there, stains on the carpet or damage to walls.

I'm ticking off – kitchen good, bathroom good, laundry good and balcony good. I'm taking my time to be sure I don't miss anything at the same time I'm watching the girls out of the corner of my eye.

During this time they've been quietly and nervously standing beside the closed door to the main bedroom.

I'm thinking 'ah huh, that's it, there's someone in the bedroom'. I slowly take my time walking in their direction, enjoying watching them squirm, after all, most midterm inspections are pretty boring.

Standing at the door I ask "is it ok to go in?".

The girls both nod their heads.

As I open the bedroom door I'm expecting to reveal 'the girls' guilty secret.

I'm playing it out in my head, I 'pounce' on my discovery of damage or another person, then I turn to 'the girls' and give them the 'Death Stare', point my finger at them and gruffly say something like "this is not allowed".

I was having some fun with them. If there was damage most of the time it can be repaired or if someone else was living in the unit we would have just advised the owner and add a note to the lease. After all it was a two bedroom unit. They were good tenants, had never been a problem.

To my slight shock there were no signs of another person or any damage throughout the entire unit.

This starts me thinking 'I've been doing this too long ..... I'm imagining things ..... Was there really all that muffled noise from inside the unit whilst I was waiting for them to open the front door?'

I complete the inspection and was walking to the living room, I decided to open the linen cupboard, one of the girls distracted me for a moment but I still had my hand on the door knob and as I open it ....

there was a loud, horrible hiss and shriek, accompanied with a chorus of yells from the girls.

The few moments of commotion was added to by my even louder yell of pain and shock.

A huge cat jumps from the top shelf of the cupboard, with claws fully extended it lands on my head and face and slides down my chest until it finally jumps off me and scurries for cover into the bedroom.

Using my folder to defend myself from the 'Mauling Cat', my paperwork had fallen all over the floor, my $200 shirt was ripped and blood is dripping from two scratches on my face.

I am not happy.

Luckily for me one of the girls was a nurse. She had a first aid kit which had some sort of solution in it that stopped cat's scratch marks from leaving permanent scars.

After we all recovered and composed ourselves, I burst out laughing, or kind of laughing with the pain from the scratches. Cat scratches really hurt. The girls were surprised that I took it all so well.

In fairness to them, they had asked me a few weeks earlier could they have a cat. I was waiting for the owner to respond. He had just returned from an overseas hiking holiday and confirmed it was ok.

Whilst I was staring at the "Mauling Cat" I told the girls the good news that the owner gave his permission for them to have a cat, but I hadn't expected them to have already acquired one.

The girls then explained the cat belonged to a friend who been rushed into hospital for an operation.

I muttered something like 'good and hoped their choice of cat would be nicer than this one.'

They laughed.

I had to return to work and explain the scratches and band-aids on my face. No one believed me.

The girls turned up at the office a few days later bringing me a new shirt, a bottle of wine and to show their new, cute kitten.

We all had a good laugh recalling the 'Mauling Cat' story to my colleagues.

Section 1: Animal Behavior

Chapter 2

Super-Dog.

We manage a pet friendly complex. It's a large complex with a lot of land and a fabulous park close by.

Whenever a unit or townhouse becomes available for sale or rent its quickly snapped up by animal lovers.

A local family with a dog were selling their home and wished to rent for six months while they looked for their next home.

As soon as they placed their home up 'For Sale' they contacted our office and put their name down to lease a two or three bed unit.

Their home sold and with absolute perfect timing an owner occupier contacted our office about the possibility of renting her unit whilst she went interstate for work.

You guessed it ....

.... for six months.

Timing was perfect, but there was one problem, it was a first floor unit and there was a dog to consider, yes a small dog but still a dog in a first floor unit – would this work?

An appointment was made for the potential tenants to view the unit, so the owner of the unit could make a decision if she was willing to allow them to live in her home for six months and with a dog.

The owner didn't mind allowing a dog, she would have had one herself, but with the long hours she worked she didn't think it was fair to a dog.

The appointment was arranged, I meet the potential tenants downstairs and take them, husband, wife, daughter and 'Jack' the dog to the unit. The owner opens the door, the wife and owner see each other and burst out laughing.

It turns out that over the last few years they had become fairly good acquaintances at the park and local shops. They hadn't seen each other for a few months as the owner had been having regular short trips interstate to set up her new position.

All parties were happy, arrangements were made.

The unit had a large balcony with a roof over a section of it and a high solid wall surrounding it. It had a great aspect as it overlooked a reserve. It was decided Jack's kennel would fit in one corner of the balcony, he would have protection from sun and rain and enough area for him to play.

Just perfect for Jack .... or so we humans thought.

The first few months all went well, but Jack got bored and started barking. After all, he was used to a yard and room to play, now he was locked on a balcony all day.

Not fair for a fun loving dog so he let anyone within hearing distance know.

Luckily with the reserve behind the unit, there weren't too many neighbors home during the day, except one.

This neighbor started putting in complaints about the barking, the owners were doing everything they could to quieten Jack, but all to no avail.

One day I received a call from the neighbor very hysterical "The dog is on the edge of the balcony, it's gonna jump. Come quickly".

Immediately I phoned the dogs owner, no answer. I had just finished showing a home around the corner so I headed to the rear of the complex.

When I reached the reserve the tenant who had called me was there looking up at the balcony.

Jack was standing on the edge of the wall barking at birds. I'm thinking crap what can I do, there's no structure that I can climb, the trees are too far away from edge of the balcony to be able to reach Jack.

By now we had created a bit of a commotion as a couple of teenagers had joined us, Jack's barking even more with the excitement.

Jack's owner was walking back from the bus stop and seeing our little circus, comes to see what's happening.

Jack sees her, barks with excitement and jumps. Someone yells "STOP", the others form a chorus of "Oohhhh......." as Jack flies through the air.

Fortunately he landed on some bushes in the garden of the unit below.

Unfortunately Jack is hurt and yelping. It looks like he's broken his leg.

I own a big six seater car, so the owner and the tenant both jump into the car and off we go to the vets with Jack whimpering.

Jack's leg gets plastered and he stays overnight in the vets.

As I'm driving everyone home, the tenant offered that Jack can stay with her during the day. After all he wouldn't be doing any more walking on the balcony wall with his leg in plaster.

The offer was gratefully accepted by the owner and I'm thinking 'Cool a problem solved by me doing a good deed.'

Over the remaining few months that Jack's owners lived at the unit, Jack was thoroughly spoilt. Living at the neighbors during the day and at home with his family at night.

The tenants found their new home, the owner occupier returned home from interstate and the neighbor put in a request with the owner of her unit for her to have a dog.

She went to a dogs home and found a dog just like Jack and gave him a good home.

Another day in a life of a Super Real Estate Agent.

Section 1: Animal Behavior

Chapter 3

Creatures That Cause Depression.

This is rather a long story about one of my own rental properties, before I became a Real Estate Agent.

A house with a self contained Granny Flat on a good size block of land. When we bought the property the Granny Flat already had a tenant living in it and was keen to stay. We had a fence put between the house and flat and a washing machine installed into the flat.

The house was rented out and all went well for a few years. We had very good income coming in from the two properties.

Time for a change of tenants in the Granny Flat.

There were a few applications for rental. The agent rang through the details, we discussed them. It came down to two applicants. As the agent had interviewed them we told him to choose one.

He chose a young male (early 20's) who was moving out of home. His parents were guaranteeing him and he had 6 weeks rent and the bond.

Even though the flat had appliances and a lounge it was not advertised as 'partly furnished'. The agent told the prospective tenant that the fridge, lounge and washing machine could stay if he wanted or could be taken away. The tenant opted for them to remain to save him the cost of buying them.

From the start there were problems.

Week one: the first call was for slugs crawling up through the bathroom vanity cupboard, he was concerned the slugs or other creatures would come into the bedroom.

A handyman went out and put some expanding caulking foam around the pipe and shelf. Twenty cents of material and $60 call out.

Week two: tenant wasn't happy, with two issues:

1. the expanding foam from last week looked untidy.

The agent asked him were there any more slugs. Tenant said no. The agent said that was the purpose of the expanding foam, if it looks untidy don't leave the door of vanity open.

2. a problem with the water draining slowly from the kitchen sink when he also was running the shower taps.

The same handyman went out, filled the kitchen sink, let it drain. All seemed fine.

He put a cloth over the shower drain, turned on the shower taps, let the tray area fill, removed the cloth and water drained away fine.

He also trimmed up the expanding foam in the vanity basin, so it didn't look so ugly.

Another $60 call out fee.

Handyman reports back to agent that both drains are draining properly. The agent reports back to tenant.

Week 3: tenant rings re: drains again and that he is an experienced plumber and the flat has been plumbed up incorrectly.

I told the agent that I would handle this and organized for the plumber who had carried out the work a few years earlier to check it out.

The plumber does the same as the handyman had previously done. I watch as the water easily drains away. He also crawled in under the flat to make sure there were no breakages in the pipes or signs of any leaking. All was good.

I ring the tenant so he could talk direct to the plumber and determine why he was complaining. The tenant tells the plumber when he has a shower and also lets the sink out at the same time they don't drain away as fast.

The plumber laughs and asks the tenant "why do you have a full kitchen sink"?

Tenant replies he fills the sink when he washes up.

Plumber than asks "how do you pull the plug on the sink when you're having a shower".

Tenant replies I run the shower before I get into it.

Plumber says "there's an easy solution, as there's a water shortage use less water when washing up. Let it drain away, then have your shower. It's not necessary to let the shower run before you get into it. Again I remind you there is a water shortage".

He then asked the tenant from where does he have plumbing experience that he feels he can make judgment about his work.

The tenant was a bit taken back with this question and mumbled about doing work experience for a week with a plumber.

In a very harsh tone the plumber replied 'that he doesn't take kindly to a teenager with a week of plumbing experience to make disparaging remarks about his work. That he has passed all his certificates and been in the trade for 25 years. If he hears any more comments about his work he will slap a defamation claim on him.'

We locked up and walked away laughing.

My bill for that call out was $100.

<u>Week 4:</u> no calls – sigh of relief.

<u>Week 5:</u> a light switch plate had cracked and was dangerous.

Fair enough an electrician replaced it.

A few weeks went by with similar small annoying issues. By now the accounts were nearly $600.

Time has rolled by and it's Christmas, that year we had a heat wave and the fridge in the flat broke down.

Unfortunately the property management were closed for the week, they did have an emergency number but the tenant for some reason didn't call it.

When the agency re-opened they told me they had a dozen calls on their machine from the tenant complaining about the fridge and ceiling fans not working fast enough.

They contacted the tenant and reminded him that the property was NOT rented as a furnished unit and he had the option when he first moved in to have his own fridge. They suggested that it may now be time to purchase his own fridge.

He said he was only staying another two months then going to work interstate and didn't want a fridge of his own.

The agent rang me for instructions. I had a spare fridge, it was old but clean and working. I arranged to take it over the next day.

Next morning when we arrive with the fridge, the tenant was home. He complained the replacement fridge wasn't a new one.

We reminded him that he wasn't paying for a furnished unit and we were bringing him this fridge as he was only staying for another two months.

He then asked for a refund of $50 per week for the whole term as he was paying too much rent.

I explained he was paying the going rent for a self contained Granny Flat with off street parking, close to the train station and gracefully declined his request of a reduction in rent and left.

Two months later he's finally ready to vacate, the agent rang and asked if I wanted the good news or bad news first.

I asked for the good news first – the agent said "the whimp" is leaving (I haven't mentioned yet the agent really disliked the tenant, he called him "the whimp").

I said good, what's the bad news?

Agent said he's taking you to The Tribunal.

I asked what for?

Agent said for the return of ALL his rent for eight months and for damages to his health.

I ask what damages to his health?

Agent replies – Depression and Dermatitis.

By now I'm starting to get angry and ask Dermatitis from what?

Agent – bird lice.

I ask - what bird lice?

Agent – the bird lice living in the eaves of the flat.

My reply – what eaves, the flat doesn't have any eaves. (I won't go into the structure of the roof and ceiling, except that there were no cavities for birds to get into). The agent agreed.

Continuing I ask - did you say Depression? Why are we responsible for 'Depression'?

Agent – well the bird lice gave him Dermatitis, which has affected his eyes, that are swollen and he can't see, so he can't go anywhere and he's 'Depressed'.

At this point I didn't know whether to laugh from the ludicrousness of it all or cry because it was such a stupid potential claim that it was likely to win in The Tribunal. As Tribunals are often more allowing to a tenant than to an investor with a property.

As the tenant was asking for ALL his rent back there was a chance that he would be awarded some kind of compensation.

The agent then tells me he's really looking forward to taking this one to The Tribunal.

Day of the tribunal, we decide not to go as we'd likely punch the guy out and really give him something to be 'Depressed' about.

Agent reports back that The Tribunal Member gave the tenant the turn to speak first.

The tenant had a large report of all the issues he found wrong with the flat including the plumbing being illegal, the fridge breaking down, the ceiling fans working slow etc. He showed a photo of his eyes swollen.

Our Property Agent had already prepared a written report about the calls and the responses from the agency and us.

The Tribunal Member allowed the tenant all the time to 'complain' about us and the agent. Then asked if he had finished.

The tenant says yes with a really sad, pouty face.

Then The Member laid down the law. The Granny Flat was rented as unfurnished for fair value to the surrounding flats, he should be appreciative of having the appliances at no extra cost. The Landlord sounds like a responsible owner who responded to every request you made even if the complaints were petty. I have pictures here of the flat, please confirm they are correct.

The tenant confirmed.

The Member continued, I agree with the agent there is no reasonable access for birds to nest in the roof area as there are no eaves. Therefore I can not accept there was any bird lice and seeing that you complained about so many other issues there are no reports here that you advised about any bird lice. Is that correct?

The tenant fumbled with an answer for this and quietly admitted he hadn't complained.

The Member replied - surely if you were that disturbed by birds or lice you would have rung about it.

Therefore I dismiss this entire case.

The agent didn't need to speak.

The tenant went off with his tail between his legs and was probably quite 'Depressed' by then.

Yay for common sense.

Section 1: Animal Behavior

Chapter 4

Ben.

Conducting the first mid term inspection for new tenants. It was a four bedroom home, we were going through the home one room at a time.

Literally I mean 'we were going through' each room because the entire family, husband, wife and three children followed me to every room.

This is a bit unusual as tenants usually sit at their kitchen table and have a cup of coffee and read the paper or sit on their lounge and watch TV, kids play Wii or X-box.

As the tenants were relatively 'new' and I was not the agent that had assisted them when they initially inspected and chose the property, therefore I had no 'relationship' with them.

Whilst they were following me through the home, I thought to myself "they must think I'm going to take something."

As we reach to the living room, through the corner of my eye I saw a mouse take off across the room.

I yell " #%*! " there's a mouse.

The tenants don't really say anything I thought they were in shock.

I said with a nervous voice, "don't worry guys it so happens our pest control guy is just around the corner". Before anything else is said, I call Terry and he tells me he can be over in a few minutes as he was just leaving his last job.

I convey this information to the tenants thinking they'd be relieved to know the fantastic service our office gives.

Instead I just get silence and unhappy faces.

True to Terry's word a few minutes later there's a knock at the door. The lady of the house is reluctant to open the door, so I open the door for her.

Then as she throws herself on the floor she grabs Terry's leg and begs him "Please don't kill, Ben".

I thought she was referring to one of her children.

But than it clicked 'Ben' was their pet mouse.

The landlord found the humorous side of this and allowed Ben to stay, providing they kept him contained in the laundry or it's cage.

Chapter 5

Ben's Friends Share A Cuppa.

We were managing a lovely old Californian Bungalow, 1930's era.

The tenants rang re: bad water pressure. I take the call and organize to attend the next day and carry out a mid-term inspection.

Next day, the tenants were right the pressure seemed really bad. I didn't remember it being like that on the previous inspection. The tenant confirmed it had only been the last week or so that they noticed it and it was getting worse.

I called our local plumber to see if he could urgently come around. He confirmed he could be there in an hour.

I finished the mid-term inspection, which on this particular property took at least half an hour (it had a pool, a huge detached garage and a granny flat at the rear which the tenants used as a work studio).

Whilst waiting for the plumber, the tenant and I walked around the perimeter of the main home to make sure there were no signs of a broken pipe.

The plumber arrives, the tenant and I finish off outside and go inside for coffee and wait for the plumbers report.

Being an old home the Hot Water System was an old style gravity feed which has a large holding tank in the ceiling.

We hear bashing and all sorts of noises and then a loud "Crikey... $%##*&". He comes back down and says "well you'll need a new Hot Water System, I'll look around for the best location and get a quote organized for you."

He pulls down his step ladder and starts to walk outside, he turns around and says "oh by the way what water did you use in the coffee?"

The tenants says from the hot water tap. The plumber very casually says "you may want to tip it out".

We look at him and ask why.

He walks over to the kitchen tap, removes the filters and begins to pull out all sorts of furry substances and fleshy matter.

With a big grin he says "there are three rats decomposing in the hot water tank, they must have fallen in and drowned. It sometimes happens with those type of old tanks".

As the plumbers words filtered into my mind, I looked into my coffee cup to see if there were any floating things in it.

There wasn't but that didn't seem to help, I started dry reaching. The tenant joined in with me.

We quickly ran over to the sink and stuck fingers down our throats. She grabbed a glass to get water from the fridge to rinse her mouth, but realized the water in the fridge had come through the same tap filter with all the gross bits in it.

I ran out to the car where I had some bottles of water. I grabbed two bottles while calling for the tenant to come outside.

Pouring the water into our mouths we gargled and spat out, drank some, gargled and spat again. She ran back inside and got some salt, poured it into the remaining water in the bottles. We gargled again.

I had this picture in my head about the decomposed rats, their intestines, skin and fur all going through my body.

My body had a big spasm, then the tenant said we've been showering and drinking that water for weeks and she had a big spasm.

Next day they had a new outside Hot Water System installed.

Their lease had just expired, the tenants gave their notice and were gone in a week.

For weeks I had pictures flashing into my mind about the black plague and skin rashes with pus oozing out of them.

This was not a good experience.

Chapter 6

Dogs Habits.

An open house was organized and nothing seemed to go right from the start.

Not to bore you with the entire list, let me tell you what happened on the day of the open. It was cloudy and some rain had already fallen.

People were arriving I was appreciative we had a turn out. I was busy attending to the outside while my colleague was taking care of everyone inside.

I noted one particular fellow had a bit of an arrogant attitude or was he just looking for a bargain? Everything was a negative for this fellow.

It got to the point where I had enough of him so I left him to his own devices. He seemed happy with this and wandered around the substantial sized back yard.

I gave my attention to an excited couple, their positive comments and outlook were refreshing and their attitude catching, I was starting to feel good again.

We stopped by the side of the house to discuss possible extensions to the garage and perhaps a pergola. The owner had looked into this just before he decided to sell the home so I was informing them of what he had learned from council and other authorities.

When, out of the blue, I hear the negative fellow say "you're full of crap" or at least that's what I thought he said.

I was starting to become angry and turned to him. He was smiling which made me even more annoyed.

In an upset tone I said "I beg your pardon."

He replied, "Mate - I'm just telling you that you're standing on crap."

I looked down and sure enough I was standing on a recently deposited pile of dogs poop.

I was so embarrassed by my outburst, I mumbled something about 'Dogs Habits' and we all laughed it off.

The home sold but not to either of these two parties.

Don't worry – I thought I'd save you the descriptive picture.

Sorry I couldn't resist including this photo, I thought it very so aptly described the story.

Chapter 7

Cat Habits.

Many years ago at the start of my Real Estate career, my role was the Customer Relations Manager for a Property Investment company.

Traditional agents would handle the sale process, then I would meet with the clients before settlement of property and make sure everything was in order. The majority of clients were first time property investors.

Often my role was an educator. Explaining tax benefits and how to keep good records so they would receive the best advantages of their new property. These meetings took between one and two hours to complete.

One particular client lived in a rural area, a one and a half hour drive away.

We were in the middle of an excessively hot summer, every day was heat wave conditions.

The morning of the meeting, I went through my wardrobe looking for something light weight, loose and comfortable as most of the afternoon I'd be sitting, with the drive there and back and the meeting. I washed the outfit and hung it out on a small stand on my back verandah.

After lunch I fell asleep, about an hour later I woke up dripping in sweat. I rushed in for a shower to freshen up and to cool down. Grabbed the clothes off the stand, got dressed and headed off to the country.

All the car windows were down to catch whatever fresh breeze there was. About half way through the drive I occasionally smelt an unpleasant odor. I thought I'm in the country with lots of animals, its a hot day, not much breeze, ok, time to put the windows up and air conditioner on.

This didn't help the smell, it was coming more often and it was getting stronger.

By this stage I was nearly at the clients property and was concentrating on the directions they had given me. I'm in their driveway, get out of the car and was greeted by two dogs who were very intent on sniffing me. I get on well with animals, but these dogs were enormous and quite overpowering, it was very hot and I wasn't in the mood to be sniffed so amorously.

The client greets me, we go into the air conditioned house, luckily the dogs are left outside.

Half way into the meeting, the distinct odor I had smelt in my car was returning. After a few minutes it was becoming embarrassingly 'on the nose, downright smelly' just like a farm yard.

Yes I was at a hobby farm with a bunch of domestic animals, but I was the common factor of my car and now inside the house.

It had to be something on me. I explained to the client what had happened in my car, excused myself to go outside and check the bottoms of my shoes.

They were clean, but the smell was worse.

The client followed me out suggesting we had a break and asked if I would like to see the new "American Barn" he had just built. We headed off to the barn, chatting about the home office he had just fitted out in the barns loft area.

As I lift my leg to climb the ladder, the odor comes back with a vengeance.

Just then the two enormous dogs come running into the barn making a bee line straight for me. I'm thinking oh boy I'm going to be their next meal, so I skimmy up the ladder. The owner orders the dogs to sit, obediently they do but their eyes are looking very longingly at me.

By now I'm sitting on the loft floor catching my breath with my legs resting on the ladder rung. Then it dawns on me what this odor is. I bend over to smell the bottoms of my pants, it was over-powering and now with my focus on the smell, it was instantly recognizable.

CAT URINE.

I remember my cat had been hanging around near the stand when I hung my clothes out to dry earlier that morning. The bottoms of the pants were very close to the ground. She must have relieved herself on them.

That's why the dogs thought I'd make a nice meal. The heat of the car, mixed with my body heat and the polyester material of the pants suit must have slowly activated, then released the extremely offensive smell of cat urine.

The client thought it was hilarious, we went back into the house to finish our meeting. He excused himself for a minute and came back with a pair of his shorts to change into, which I gladly accepted.

My pants were thrown into the garbage.

We were sitting at the kitchen table finishing our meeting when his wife walks in. The client introduces us, the wife gives me a very strange look, probably thinking who is this lady wearing my husbands shorts.

The story is quickly explained, I finish my meeting and gladly say good-bye, promising to mail the shorts back to him.

As I'm walking to my car I assume he told his wife the story of my smelly pants and the excited dogs, because I hear laughter coming from the house.

That's good, it's nice to leave a meeting knowing everyone is happy.

I was relieved as I had a clear passage to my car, no dogs to attack and devour me.

Thankfully the drive home was not as smelly.

It however was splattered with out bursts of my laughter as I recalled the last few hours and thinking of all the things I'd do to my cat when I got home.

FunnyShortStoriesBy.com

Section 2

The "X – Rated" Section

Bodies Exposed.

FunnyShortStoriesBy.com

Section 2 – Bodies Exposed

Chapter 8

Gorgeous Blonde Surprised.

A few years ago I had a open house, my first lookers were two young couples in their late 20's. One of the girls was tall, gorgeous with long blonde hair dressed in a very short mini skirt and long black boots.

Not the usual type of garb or person who inspects houses, at least not the types of houses I sell.

After going through the house the guys ended up out the back checking out a large brick workshop with an inspection pit and the works. A real guys 'shed'.

We then moved back to into the house through the laundry...."Oh by the way here is the second toilet" and I proceeded to swing the door wide open. Imagine our faces as we three guys make eye contact with the gorgeous blonde ....

sitting on the toilet enjoying her few moments of peace until we rudely interrupt her .

I really didn't know if I should laugh or cry .... apologizing I quickly close the door.

Fortunately the boy friend and his mate went off with a smile on their faces.

Me, I had a chuckle but can still feel the red face of embarrassment!

FunnyShortStoriesBy.com

Section 2 – Bodies Exposed

Chapter 9

A Perfect Open.

For sale a two level, two bedroom, two bathroom unit. The unit is tenanted. Having a tenant in a property while it's for sale is different to having an owner living in the property. The owner has a vested interest to keep it clean and tidy and generally prepared for an 'open' so the agent can present their property at its best (hopefully).

Having a tenant living in the property generally adds an extra bit of effort for the agent, as we have to encourage the tenant to maintain the property in an acceptable condition.

In a lot of cases this acceptable condition is above how the tenant generally lives. In addition we need to set a time for the opens when the tenant will not be home but is also a standard time that buyers expect opens to be available to view.

Usually there is no benefit in the sale transaction for the tenant, as they know there is a high likelihood they'll have to leave once the sale is completed.

Some tenants even sabotage a sale, therefore the agent must handle these type of transactions very skillfully.

Back to the unit I'm listing for sale with a tenant.

The tenant has lived in this very popular complex for a year and they don't want to leave. They have allowed key access at set times.

A standard start to the day, the office has carried out the usual confirmations, email and phone calls to both tenants, the day before and one hour before open. The morning of the open neither tenant answered their cell phones or the home phone. Messages were left on all.

It's Saturday morning 10.10 am, I buzz the unit at the entrance to complex, no answer. I proceed to the unit and knock loudly on the door, no answer. I open the door and call out the tenants names, again no answer.

I'm happy the tenants are out, it's now 10:15 am and the open is for 10.30, so I start to prepare the unit to show it.

I open all the blinds, turn on the air conditioner as well as the exhaust fans in kitchen and downstairs bathroom to ventilate the unit.

Turn on the radio and change the channel to find some nice, relaxing music.

The kitchen - I clean up and place the dishes and cutlery in their appropriate areas, put away a few packs of food that are on the bench top and wipe down the bench.

The bathroom - I pick up the towels off floor, fold them neatly on towel rail, flush the toilet and put the lid down, give the sink and bench a wipe over.

The living room and second bedroom – only require a quick tidy.

Whilst I'm doing all this I'm not exactly quiet, some cupboard doors have been banging, some plates have been clicking together as I put them away. I start singing to a "golden oldie" song that's playing on the radio.

Now I'm ready for the upstairs which has the master bedroom, en-suite and study area.

Still singing I run up the stairs, two steps at a time, turn on the light, walk towards the en-suite to repeat what I have just done downstairs, turn on exhaust fan, tidy towels etc.

Through the corner of my eye I notice something I wasn't expecting, I freeze and take in the scene, this is the first time this has ever happened to me ………

The bed is occupied, there are two naked bodies on the bed, peacefully asleep.

There is clothing strewn across the floor and a bottle of champagne and two glasses on the bedside table.

I quickly proceed to turn off the bedroom light and go down the stairs, quietly this time. Collect my bag and left the unit.

I made up a sign to put on the foyer door that said

"Sorry OPEN closed for the day"

and waited outside the main entrance to greet the potential buyers who attended, giving them some lame excuse why they couldn't inspect the unit today.

Of course I took their details to organize another time for them attend.

On the way to the next property I had time to reflect.

Remembering in my rush to vacate I forgot to turn off the en-suite light and exhaust fan and downstairs the radio was still playing, air conditioner and exhaust fans running and their kitchen and bathroom were much tidier than what they had left it in the night before.

I wondered if the tenants would notice this when they woke up.

Nothing was ever said between myself and the tenants, I imagine they were a bit embarrassed.

In the following weeks after this episode, when I had the opens, I found the unit was always tidy with the air conditioner and exhaust fans running, the radio turned on and the kitchen, bathrooms and bedrooms tidy. And no tenants to be seen, anywhere.

After this experience each open was perfect, the unit was sold to an investor, the tenants continue to live there.

A happy ending for everyone.

Now when I hold opens I go through the entire property first before I do my general tidy up. Just to be sure.

FunnyShortStoriesBy.com

Chapter 10

Property Sold
And A Divorce.

An agent working for me was selling a home.

It was arranged with the owners to have key access and to be able to show the home at any time, just to call them in advance so they could tidy up if necessary.

On this particular day, a Saturday about 1pm, a gentlemen walks into the office and wishes to see the home straight away. He needed a home quickly as his work was relocating him.

This property was close to a particular school he wanted his children to attend, close to his work and other facilities.

He was what agents consider a "dream buyer".

69

As our office had held an "open for inspection" earlier that morning we knew the home was tidy and presentable.

Our agent called both the owners cell phones and home phone, no answer, he left messages on all phones.

About 15 minutes later the potential buyer and agent arrive at the house, ring the door bell and as there is no answer they go in.

The agent takes the potential buyer on the tour of the home. He was keen to see the backyard first, then the kitchen. Explaining his children would love the backyard and his wife the kitchen, if they were happy, he would be happy. At this point everything was perfect.

A few minutes later it's time for the bedrooms.

Our agent and potential buyer were having a good chat whilst walking up the hall. They reach the main bedroom, the agent casually opens the door and stops mid way. To his amazement.......................

there are two people lost in each others pleasures.

He quickly shuts the door, explains the situation to the potential buyer and they leave.

They return to the office. Luckily the episode didn't wane the clients interest in the home. They arrange a second viewing for his family to attend and he leaves.

The agent tells me the story so I'm aware of what has happened.

About an hour later the receptionist takes a call from one of the owners of the home.

I quickly take the call and with great nervousness begin to explain why Michael, my agent, took the buyer through the house.

The vendor says no problem they were his instructions he just wanted to know what the outcome was.

I say to the owner with a tone of confusion, "I'm sorry that Michael walked in on you in the bedroom, but he stopped the potential buyer at the door so he didn't see anything. They decided to leave and made another appointment .... etc" finishing with "we're really sorry that we barged in ....".

Before I could finish, the owner says "mate what are you talking about, did you do the inspection or not, I've been at work since 8am and just finished, I just got the message".

The potential buyer bought the home, it ended up being a very quick and easy settlement so the divorce could go through.

I wouldn't say this was the perfect ending for all, or maybe it was!

Chapter 11

Pirates And Lesbians.

An agent was selling a charming "settlers" cottage. Real Estate prices were unfortunately dropping at the time and sales were slow.

Buyers were certainly not snapping up properties. A classic 1890 two bedroom cottage located 1.5km from the city, surrounded with trendy cafes, is normally in big demand, but we were struggling to bring in lookers.

Like many other hopeful vendors, the owners spent endless weekends painting, tiling, puttying, trimming and cleaning to have their home perfect for the proposed sale.

After sprucing the cottage up complete with a striking, glossy red front door, the 'For Sale' sign went up and the open home commenced.

The vendors did everything right, every Saturday cleaning and polishing, bowls of fresh flowers everything was spotless.

The only problem was the young student neighbors, and boy oh boy, were they a problem.

They were not in the spirit of the sale process, leaving their lower rear deck littered with empty bottles and rubbish from the festivities of the night before.

The vendors approached them and asked very nicely if they could just tidy up a bit prior to the Saturday open homes.

This request was not only ignored but their behavior worsened by adding a large 'Jolly Roger' Pirate flag across the wall of their deck that provided a small screen between the two properties.

The Jolly Roger flag was flown by pirates with the intention of creating fear in the victims.

Not the best symbol for a prospective buyer to see from the deck, which was the best selling feature of this little cottage.

The owners asked if the flag could be removed just for the Saturday opens. It seems every request was met with more "attitude" by the young neighbours.

I placed a call to the managing agent as one professional to another. But was advised that, 'It is a tenants' right to decorate their home in whatever manner they choose and was not something that they can control.

So we all soldiered on, Saturday after Saturday.

We were coming to the end of our agency agreement, this was our last open and finally we have an interested buyer.

As usual after the open I would ring the owners and update them. This particular call was a difficult one.

"I don't quite know how to tell you this", I said.

"What? What's wrong, what's happened?"

"I did have one group through who were really interested. They loved the cottage. They said it was perfect for them".

The owners picked up on my negative word.

"You said 'were' interested - I bet it was that darn flag and the smell of beer and cigarettes on the deck next door that put them off!".

"No", not really" I said. "That didn't seem to bother them, but they were somewhat taken aback by
....

the two young girls next door 'making out' on the neighbors deck in full view of everyone".

"They seemed to be putting on a show for us".

The owners ended up renting the home for six months. Luckily the Pirate and Lesbian neighbors moved.

Six months later the owners put the home up for sale at just the right time.

The home sold in a few weeks at a price they were very happy with.

Chapter 12

Men Can Look Sexy In An Apron.

We had a tenant with a very full home. They were leasing a two bedroom unit for over 2.5 years.

In this time the family had grown from two adults and two toddlers to two adults and four toddlers (all boys). All within the ages of 6 months (twins) to four years.

OMG.

The owner decides he wants to sell the property and we had to prepare the unit for sale.

The previous inspection was six months earlier and the lady of the home was about five months pregnant. So this inspection we were expecting to be a bit different.

Pre-sale inspection time, the place was a mess, but nothing our expert team couldn't fix.

Luckily, the wife and the children were scheduled to fly overseas to visit the grand parents for five weeks.

Great opportunity to help the husband clean up and prepare the unit for sale.

Two weeks later the time came and we sent the teams in to clean and do some touch up paint work preparing for the photos and the video.

Our decorator stayed back making the final touches as the photographers were arriving later in the afternoon.

Meanwhile the husband arrived home and with wide eyes says to our decorator "My god, I don't recognize the place. I actually realize how untidy we have been living. I will have to talk to my wife when she gets back"

Two weeks later the wife arrives home.

As we are the main managing agent of this complex, we are on friendly terms with the majority of the owners and tenants.

One of the neighbors reported when the wife returned home, that it was like a circus coming into town. With family members helping bring in the troop of boys. The strollers, luggage, new toys to show off.

The boys are excited to be home and see Dad, friends and neighbors. It was a noisy, funny and exciting.

But it wasn't long before ....

WHAM!!! KAPOW**** OMG+++++

.... there was a big 'domestic' (argument) between the husband and his wife.

Apparently the wife took objection to a comment from the husband about her cleaning habits.

With a lot of comments about what does he think she does all day, sit on her A.. and watch TV?

The last time I was there for an inspection, the husband was vacuuming the unit and he actually had an apron on.

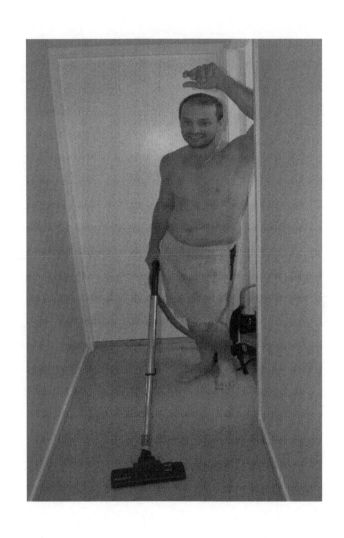

Section 3

Every Good Book About Property Has a Tale About Landlords and Owners

Section 3 – Tales About Landlords and Owners

Chapter 13

The Nigerian Money Scam.

I had just started my new role in Property Management. The Licensee (Mr. A.) asked me to attend a lunch meeting he had with a Landlord (Mrs. G).

He had just received an emergency call from her that she needed to meet with him regarding an urgent matter that couldn't be discussed over the phone.

As we walked to our meeting he gave me some background on the Landlord.

She had been widowed for about a year, was in her mid sixties, no children, she was partners with her late husband in a small Mortgage Brokering business but not done any business since her husband passed away and she was financially well to do.

In the past Mr. A and Mrs. G. had referred some business to each other. He was hoping that I might form a connection with her and possibly encourage her back into her Mortgage Brokering Business.

How wrong was he.

We met at a restaurant, I'm introduced, we sat down.

Before we even looked at the menus Mrs. G. commenced her very long story. I was dumb struck that she was so open to tell the story in front of me, a complete stranger.

What follows is a summary of our very unusual lunch meeting.

Mrs. G. had fallen in love. He was a very dapper English Businessman (Mr. S.) in his early fifties, they met online and had been communicating for three months. He was a widower with two teenage children. The children had their nanny who had looked after them for many years as a lot of his business was international, mostly in Africa.

Alarm bells were going off by now.

He had a multi-million dollar deal that had been put on hold whilst he was dealing with his wifes' estate. However, it was necessary for him to travel to Africa to complete the deal, this would take a few months. After that he would bring his children and nanny out to visit her and really "commence their relationship".

Mr. S warned Mrs. G. the area he was traveling to was dangerous and had very poor communication systems and he may not be in touch with her for about week. This was two weeks ago and she told us all the worries and anxiety she had been experiencing for the last week not hearing from him.

This brings us to the day of our meeting.

Mrs. G. received an urgent email from Mr. S.

The email advised he had been involved in a serious car accident, his body guard had been killed and he had a broken leg and arm, chest and head injuries. He was in a rural hospital that had no services to deal with his severe injuries. He really hated to impose on their new relationship, but he needed $12,300 to cover all medical transport costs back to England, otherwise he would die.

There was no one he could depend on in such short notice.

She immediately sent the money.

The look that passed between Mr. A and myself would have been interesting to capture on video.

Mr. A. asked how long ago had she sent the money.

Mrs. G. replied a week ago and without even stopping for breath she continued in a very distressed manner. She had received an email from him the night before saying he had arrived safely in England, thanked her so much for her faith and trust in him, that he was doing as well as could be expected considering all his severe injuries and would be in touch soon. That he would repay her as soon as this multi-million dollar deal completed.

Then she received an email that morning which was why she was so distressed. A nurse from the hospital Mr. S. was at, emailed her and said Mr. S. had asked her to send an email to advise Mrs. G. to prepare herself for bad news, that he might pass away in the next 48 hours, as his condition had worsened.

The only thing that would save Mr. S. was a very expensive operation, he needed $9,500 for this operation but he could not get the funds together fast enough.

Mr. A. interrupted and asked had she sent the money.

Mrs. G. reply was no.

Mr. A asked why was she desperate to want meet with him today.

Mrs. G. said she was scared that Mr. S. might die and she'd be alone again and should she go to England to help him.

Mr. A. asked is this really why she wanted to meet with him.

Mrs. G. said of course, what other reason would there be.

Mr. A. in his wisdom replied, "if you truly believed his story, you would not have hesitated to be on a plane or to send the money".

Mrs. G. denied this and that "she was looking for help to organize everything and to make sure her two properties would be looked after whilst she was away etc".

Mr. A. assured her that her properties are always well looked after and had she spoken to anyone else about this situation.

Mrs. G. confided she had spoken with a close girl friend who said she was being scammed and not to send any money or travel anywhere.

Mr. A asked was she going to take her friends advice.

Mrs. G. said she didn't know and started to cry.

Mr. A. said that he needed to be back at the office, he wished her all the best with whatever decision she made, assured her that her properties would be in good hands and asked me to walk Mrs. G. back to the car and to return to the office as soon as possible.

I did as requested and heard more of her story on the walk to the car. She was lonely, she had no one she could trust, she was quite willing to send the money if she thought he (Mr. S.) was going to marry her. That her late husband made all the decisions and all she wanted was someone to tell her what to do. Could I help her.

As I bid her farewell, I suggested that she already had two opinions from a friend and a colleague, that maybe she should really listen to what they had suggested.

Back at the office, Mr. A. said he had already received two phone calls from Mrs. G. asking for assistance and information.

For the readers thinking did Mrs. G. send the money. Yes she did.

Over the next month she received another three emails, always with a story attached and asking for more money. Almost every day she emailed or phoned Mr A. to update him on the saga.

Mr A. sent a memo out to all staff members, that no one was to engage in any form of correspondence with Mrs. G. That everything was to be referred to him. It was a very difficult situation and needed to be handled with care and tact.

Mr. A. believed that when Mrs. G came to reality she would be looking for someone to blame.

Mr A. then organized to hand the management over to another agent, telling me it was costing him too much for THERAPY.

FunnyShortStoriesBy.com

Section 3 – Tales About Landlords and Owners

Chapter 14

She Treats Me Like A God – Burnt Offerings.

You've heard the stories about making prospective buyers 'feel at home' at opens by roasting coffee, baking a cake or bread, even having a roast cooking in the oven.

Well this story is about the one that didn't go as planned.

A lot of years ago when I was the new kid in our team, I was keen to prove myself.

The licensee gave me a Real Estate Agents magazine. I read it from cover to cover, devouring the tips and ideas.

I particularly took to heart the story of creating the emotional triggers of family and home to sell the property i.e. the smell of freshly baked bread or a roast dinner. Smells that conjure up comfort and happiness, even love.

I talked it over with my first vendor.

She thought it was a great idea and decided on the cake.

A typical women, a multi-tasker. She could create the desired atmosphere at the same time have a fresh cake and tea after the open house and we could discuss how the open went.

All set ready to go.

A nice three bedroom home in the suburbs, great yard for kids, plenty of room to extend the home. And a cake cooking in the oven.

The "emotion triggers" of home and family were working well, at least for me as I remembered when Mum baked a cake for me and my big sister. When it was cooked and slightly cooled she'd call us inside to have cake and milk.

Great memories.

The cake smelled wonderful, my mouth was watering thinking of fresh cake and now that I was more mature my preference was for coffee instead of milk.

Let's see how if it works with potential buyers.

Jackpot.

We got a bite on the first go, a lady fell in love with the home, she called her husband.

He was just finishing work and could come over in about 15 minutes.

As this was my first solo open I had the time to wait. So I chatted with the lady buyer, how long had they been looking, did they have kids, what did they do for work etc.

Just as the intending buyers husband walks in the front door, the smoke alarm goes off.

The vendor was in the back yard waiting for the open to finish. She hears the alarm go off and rushes into the kitchen as she yells "OOOhhh NO - we forgot the cake".

As smoke fills the room she pulls out the blackened cake, the piercing scream of smoke alarm is still ringing in our ears.

Just like an expert she places the cake tin in the sink and runs the tap over it, opens all the doors and windows to let the smoke out.

Just then her husband walks in the back door, expecting the open to be finished. He turns to the potential buyers and me and says "My wife treats me like a God, she always serves me burnt offerings"

We all have a good laugh.

As we said our goodbyes to the owners, I noticed the potential buyers were looking up at the ceiling. They asked if there had been any fires in the home.

Section 3 – Tales About Landlords and Owners

Chapter 15

Time Warp.

As a Licensee, one of my new recruits comes in all excited talking about the new listing he just got, it was a very strong referral from his aunt.

I give him some last minute coaching before he makes "The Call" to the owner for the appointment.

All goes well, Mrs Young the owner was home and available for us to go over and meet with her. David and I head on out to the property.

The street appeal of the house had a lot going for it: elevated block, district views, a nice brick veneer home.

We ring the door bell and we're greeted by Mrs Young. She asks us in.

The hall way was dark, it takes a few moments for my eyes to adjust. Whilst they're adjusting I notice what appears to be piles of stuff, lots of piles, in fact as my eyes adjust it was a room full of piles.

Mrs Young leads us down a very well formed walkway. We walk single file as it was just wide enough for one person to comfortably walk down.

Every available space was used, the only floor area was the walkway, along both walls of the hall were stacks of books, magazines or newspapers all meticulously stacked to chest height.

The higher sections of the walls had framed pages from newspapers of historical events - landing on the moon, Nelson Mandela, President Kennedy's assassination, Queen Elizabeth's Coronation, Princes Charles and Princess Diana's wedding, the birth of Prince William and Prince Harry (she obviously loved the royals).

This walk was like going through a Time Warp.

It was a very slow walk, as David and I take in this amazing scene. Being a movie buff I liken it to being in the dark basement of a museum where centuries of books and newspapers are stored for prosperity.

We reach the lounge room and Mrs Young, points to the lounge for us to sit.

My new recruit, David, looks at me. I'm sure we both had the same look of bewilderment on our faces.

A myriad of thoughts are going through my mind, this situation had to be handled very tactfully, because what I thought less than a minute ago was, look at all this 'rubbish' .... she's obviously too old to clean this up, we'll have to get in a rubbish bin and a couple of guys to move all this .... whats the rest of the house like ....

Mrs Young breaks my thoughts by asking would we like a cup of tea or coffee, I welcome the interrupt as we organize our drinks. She disappeared into the kitchen, I looked at David and asked him what he thought?

David didn't know what to say, his look of shock and disillusionment said it all, he was still seeing a mess and a difficult sale. He told me later he couldn't think of anything positive to say.

Sitting on the lounge I saw a different scene, everything is neat, orderly and clean. All these piles of stuff appears to be treasured memorabilia of this elderly lady. Beside the lounge where I sat were two shorter piles of newspapers with lace doilies on the top.

Just then Mrs Young returns with tea and biscuits, she had obviously organized this before we arrived. She put them down on the two short piles with the doilies.

That answered the question I had in my mind about what their purpose was. They were interesting side tables.

I began by saying, Mrs Young, I hear you are looking at selling.

"Yes, I have a lot of respect for David's Aunt, she highly recommends your agency".

I smile and nod, like a good apprentice David copies me.

Mrs Young explains she wanted to retire and the upkeep of two homes was just too much for her. I continued to smile and nod.

Mrs Young continues "I have decided to sell my other home, then I can reduce my hours and dedicate more time to .... (she spreads her arms apart) my reading".

David's face once again lights up as he realizes it wasn't THIS home she wanted to sell but a rental home she had close by.

What a relief.

Her other property was a lovely well looked after home. It sold quickly for a great price. A young couple who wanted to start a family fell in love with it.

Mrs Young was a very interesting lady, she had been a highly sort after curator for a host of museums during her fifty plus years of work.

Soon after the home settled Mrs Young retired from work and started living her dream, doing lots of reading and writing.

She is now a successful author with her books published on Amazon and Kindle. The funny thing is with all the research material she has available at her finger tips her forte was not what we expected.

In fact she specialized in a very unusual field, especially for a gray-haired elderly lady.

Romance and Erotica novels.

It just goes to show, the old saying in this occasion was very apt...........

'You can't judge a book by its cover'.

This is the satisfying part of our work with all parties extremely happy.

We assist with life changing experiences for all.

A happy ending to our Time Warp experience.

Section 4

The Essential Love Story

Chapter 16   Fred and Ginger

Conclusion:

About The Authors:

Photo Resources:

FunnyShortStoriesBy.com

Section 4 – The Essential Love Story.

Chapter 16

Fred and Ginger.

It's Monday morning, our weekly meeting of all staff and agents to review the previous week and in particular the weekend activities. These meetings are pretty standard and routine. Someone usually has a funny story or two to recite to the team.

About two years ago something happened to change the atmosphere of these meetings. In fact an award and prize was created for "The Best Story" of the month because of the following.

Before our meeting commenced I opened the mail. One letter was from a Body Corporate of a unit block where we managed some units. This letter was an official complaint from the body corporate. The letter went along the lines of .... "a number of complaints have been made to our office re: Unit 69, 1 Hot St, (address changed to protect the tenants). The complaints are for *"**excessively amorous nocturnal activities**"*. Please ensure you immediately contact your tenants and ensure this situation is corrected".

I read the very short letter, stopped and had to re-read it again for it to sink into my brain. Then I burst out laughing.

As a Real Estate Agent of nine years, this was the first time I'd experienced such a letter.

I also study law, so my student brain takes over for a moment, I grab my trusty "Lawbook of Cases and Materials" looking for any cases involving a similar situation. There was none.

Then I switch my brain back to Real Estate Agent, thinking who is this lucky young "amorous couple" that I'll need to have a meeting and chat with.

I check the address on the letter, picture myself at the property.

We had only recently re-let this unit so the tenants faces immediately popped into my mind and I'm flabbergasted.

I'm so shocked that I call our receptionist to check the database and confirm who the tenants are. She buzzes me on the intercom and confirmed what I knew.

All I could think was, WOW!.

Then I recall that the tenants were very adamant that they wanted a twelve month lease.

We all go into our meeting, we come to the news section, I let everyone tell their standard news. Then I advise that I had received a very serious letter from a Body Corporate and with these type of situations we must act on them immediately.

I commenced reading the short letter word for word, very slowly.

The team were unsure what to do, say or probably even think, until one of the more senior members, Bruce, started laughing with his huge belly laugh. This broke the tension in the others who joined with him. The chorus of laughter was extremely loud and very contagious. Only stopped long enough for someone to make a rather suggestive comment which started everyone off again.

I'm sure it would be a professional comedian's dream to have so much non-stop laughter. One lady colleague had to excuse herself to go to the bathroom before she had an accident.

When I brought the team to some sort of control, I continued with the news of describing the tenants, everyone was .... stunned.

Stunned is probably the closest descriptive word I can come up with as I recall seeing the individual faces frozen in time as they each conjured up their own experiences mixed with their own sense of humour.

You see, the tenants were a gray haired couple in their early seventies.

At the time the husband Fred was 72 and wife Ginger was 71. (fictitious names to protect the innocent)

Our office had or tried to have a very 'serious discussion' on how I was going to break the news to this 'amorous' elderly couple that some neighbours were complaining about their "nocturnal activities".

There was a particular question asked "how often are we talking about – once a month maybe?".

I thought it was a great question and important to know as many facts as I could before contacting Fred and Ginger. I also thought this would be an interesting training exercise on communication with other professionals we deal with.

To be totally honest the team would have drawn and quartered me if I didn't find out more in their presence.

As the phone was being set up, I did something really silly, I asked the team if they could think of any other important questions I should ask.

It took half an hour for me to bring them under control. I had to threaten them with kicking them out of the room if they didn't settle down.

Finally everyone is calm and I make the phone call. As I hadn't spoken with the writer of the letter, Jen, before I did the usual introductions, good training for the team, then I asked about the letter.

Well, Jen burst out laughing which started the team off again.

Finally I get to ask Jen about how many complaints they'd received and did she have any information that could assist me when I went to speak to the tenants.

Jen advised the complaints had come from the owners on either side of unit 69. Giggling explodes when number 69 is mentioned.

I stare at everyone for them to behave, as this is a professional call. Jen continues to explain that the owners had never complained about anything previously, so it was not like they were the 'professional complainers'.

That it had only been over the last month or so and finally she advised the "amorous nocturnal activities" were every night.

The team had been listening intently, I'm sure they were learning heaps about conducting a professional conversation – NOT – they just wanted the juicy bits.

When the team heard "every night" again they were stunned.

Bruce breaks the silence when he repeats back "EVERY NIGHT - ?%&*" you can put in your own four letter word, as a couple of words would suit and they were all used by our team.

Tom our 'office stud' then quipped up "I don't even get it that much" and the team breaks into fits of laughter again.

I said to Jen that I thought I should explain a few things to her :

1) that I was allowing our team to listen in as a training exercise

2) that the team were a bit over excited because none of us with all our years of experience had heard of this type of complaint before

3) the tenants had only moved in six weeks earlier, and finally

4) that the tenants were in their early seventies

It was Jen's turn to be silent for a few seconds, then we heard a hand go over the phone mouth piece and for a few minutes very faint laughter splattered with coughing.

During this time the team started muttering things like "I wonder if my parents (or grandparents – depending on the age of the team member) 'Do It' every night" or "my parents don't even talk, let alone 'get into it' even once a year" or just plain and simple "OMG".

Finally Jen gets back on the phone and excuses herself, saying she's never had an experience like this before and she's been in the industry for twenty five years.

That the neighbors had neglected to tell her how old the tenants were (not that it really makes any difference).

Finally that she can't wait until she goes outside and tells her colleagues.

As I had the very real problem of talking with the tenants I asked Jen did she know of any specific bi-law they would invoke if necessary?

Her reply was no, that she would have to look into it.

Our normal twenty to thirty minute meeting had taken nearly two hours, but it was two hours of fun that brought an extra spark and comradeship to our team.

Time for the phone call to the tenants, I advise the team I was making the call from my office. The team try to bribe me to make it from the meeting room.

The appointment is made to meet with the tenants. As they were both retired it was arranged for that afternoon.

For hours I'm rehearsing all these scenarios in my head, I say this, they say that. Is it really them or do they have a grandchild living with them, if so the grandchild will have to either stop or leave as they weren't listed on the lease, etc.

It's the afternoon. I knock on the door, they invite me in. They have their coffee table full of wonderful cakes and biscuits with the tea cups all ready for the brew and some glasses that were filled with what they described as 'their elixir'.

What an enlightening meeting.

They took pity on me, to save me the awkwardness of starting the conversation, they started it for me by asking had I received a letter or phone call.

To say I was shocked would be an understatement, I said yes I had received a letter that morning.

They said they were expecting it and apologised. They went on to explain they had been asked to leave their last premises because the people were "old fuddy duddy's" and they hoped that I wasn't.

This lightened the situation and allowed me to explain it wasn't up to me, I was just the messenger, so don't shoot me.

That the neighbouring owners had their rights to a good nights sleep. To which they agreed and said that they sleep very well. We all had a laugh.

Fred and Ginger went on to explain their story.

They had been engaged when they were in their late teens, her parents didn't approve of Fred and took her away to England and forbid Ginger to make any form of contact to Fred.

All she could do was write him a very brief letter saying she changed her mind about them, that she was going away and for him not to try and find her.

Being a good daughter she did as she was asked. But secretly pined for Fred.

She went to University and completed a degree in Psychology and eventually married to a wonderful man and had two children. Her husband passed away when he was 59.

She had been widowed a few years when her parents passed away and left her a letter apologising for what they made her do all those years ago, as they knew she never really got over it.

This got her to thinking about Fred. Every day something would pop into her mind about the good times they had experienced.

She kept dismissing it thinking it was a silly schoolgirl crush that she was creating in her mind. She also felt some guilt as she had a wonderful marriage and felt like she was "cheating" on her husband.

Fred told his story on how devastated he was by Gingers letter, so many unanswered questions and emotions. He tried to find her, but never thought of looking overseas for her. Eventually time diminished his

111

pain, but this experience was a determining factor for him which led him into also studying Psychology.

He eventually married and had three children. His choice of partner wasn't as good as Gingers and he divorced.

Fred said he often recalled times with Ginger and wondered what she was doing. But his heart carried some pain with it still, as Ginger had left him. For all these years he thought that she had left to get away from him.

As destiny so deemed, both their studies in Psychology took them onto being Sex Therapists. Fred in Sydney and Ginger in London.

They were both considered the experts in their fields and nearly six years earlier were invited to be guest lecturers at a symposium being held in New York. They both accepted.

In the symposiums details Gingers' name was listed as Mrs. G. Smith. When Fred read the information of course this didn't mean anything to him.

When Ginger read the information she never thought that Professor F. Jones could be Fred.

Six months later they're both in New York, Ginger is sitting in the front row of the symposium when the M.C. introduces Professor Frederick Jones. As Ginger had often thought of Fred, hearing the name brought Fred's teenage smiling face leaping into head.

She looks up and sees the same smiling face,

maybe a bit sad and forty years older, but still that smile that had melted her heart when she was eighteen.

At that moment she realised that she had never forgotten Fred. Her heart knew.

So what does any proper English lady do, she feints. Right there in the front row.

When she comes to, she finds herself on the floor with Fred kneeling over her, holding her hand like a true gentleman.

She whispers "Fred, it's you".

Fred, being an Aussie bloke, is a bit slow to catch on, smiles sweetly and says "Yes I'm Fred and you are?"

Ginger whispers "Fred, it's me, Ginger".

Fred's heart starts thumping, he leans forward and gently lifts her shoulders and hugs her. Ginger has recovered from the initial shock and hugs back with tears streaming down her cheeks.

As I'm listening to them recalling that moment, I had tears welling in my eyes.

They continued, they don't know how long they were hugging each other for, but they were told it was like a beautiful scene from the best romance movie as the audience of Psychologists burst out clapping.

They were later told that members of the audience were so moved with what they saw, that they started hugging each other, some even had tears in their eyes, just like I had.

Fred and Ginger never saw this, as they only had eyes for each other, almost forty years later.

The M.C. took them to a private room and returned to start the symposium.

He started with "How do you top that? I don't know what happened just then, but it was beautiful." The audience agreed by clapping and cheering. "I hope we find out the story before our symposium comes to a climax". Using the work "climax" in this circumstance brought a lot of laughs.

"So lets begin".

In the meantime, Fred and Ginger are in their private room, telling each others story of heart break from forty years earlier.

With a lot more hugging and even some kissing. The spark was still there, according to Ginger, "well and truly there". She quickly broke down Fred's wall of pain, of thinking he had been dumped.

Their experience had led them into the same careers on the opposite side of the world, which eventually brought them together again. It was deemed for their destinies to join - when the time was right.

The time had come and this time no one was going to stop them.

~~~~~~~~~~~~~

Now, five years later they are still making up for lost time with their "amorous nocturnal activities".

As their five children lived in different countries, Fred and Ginger travelled the world to visit them and stayed close to each child for a period of time.

Fred confessed they were asked to leave their last rental. According to them "the agent was very bombastic and didn't have a romantic bone in his body" continuing with "they were pleased to see I was a very sexy Latin American and that I would fully understand their sexual desires".

They set me up very well, where could I go after that, I certainly wasn't going to be the one to spoil their fun.

With my law studies I knew to answer a question with question. I asked them with their experience as Sex Therapists if a couple came to them with the problem of regularly being asked to leave their rental homes because of their night time sexual activity, what would they do to help them.

They loved this approach, Ginger took a note pad and pen from the dresser and commenced a list. I just drank my cup of coffee and munched on the cake whilst they came up with some very interesting ideas.

One of the suggestions was to invite the neighbours in for morning or afternoon tea and share their story as they had just unveiled to me.

I didn't know how this would work but nodded.

The very interesting thing I noticed whilst they were jotting down their ideas was not one of the suggestions mentioned to reduce the amount of their sexual activity.

In fact one of their items on the list was they could alter some of their day time activities so they could change their "amorous nocturnal activity" around to when the neighbours were at work.

What a couple!

To finish off our talk, they promised they would have the situation corrected immediately and if I could report back to the Body Corporate their apologies and that there would be no further complaints.

They really wanted to stay in the area for the year to spend time with Fred's son as he was a Psychologist.

He was at the symposium five years earlier and had witnessed their 'love story' and they hadn't spent any time with him since.

They thanked me for my time and assistance. They drank their glasses of 'elixir' and encouraged me to drink mine.

They announced they would take this to their bedroom and continue to work on it.

I got the hint.

As I was driving home I had this sudden urge to ring my wife and announce "Honey, I'm coming home early".

The next morning all the team were waiting for me in the meeting room, eagerly wanting to hear what happened.

I recalled the story. Everyone had a tears in their eyes.

Tom (the office stud) immediately asked could he

organise for a dozen bottles of the 'elixir'.

To finish a very long story. A few weeks later I rang Fred and Ginger to see how things were going.

Ginger told me that they had their afternoon tea with the neighbours, told them their story as they told me a few weeks earlier.

That one of the wives broke down into uncontrollable crying and said how their marriage was on the rocks and they hadn't had sex for more than a year. That she loved her husband but he was always at work and she felt so alone ....

The other couple joined in with their marital problems.

Fred and Ginger offered their expertise, they commenced regular Sex Therapy sessions assisting the couples to return to a loving relationship.

When the time was right they shared with them the 'elixir', now all of them are enjoying "amorous nocturnal activities".

Oh what a happy ending .... and hopefully the perfect ending to our book.

Have an enjoyable night.

Notes:

maybe your own marketing ideas

Notes:

more marketing ideas

Conclusion:

We hope you have enjoyed our combination of Funny Short Stories and that they have brought some enjoyment to your life, and that maybe one day if you're feeling a bit down, that a story or a picture may just pop into your mind and bring a smile to your face.

If you're one that likes to share your fun, you might pass this book onto a friend or colleague.

Maybe even share your own stories.

If you would like to share your story with us go to **http://untold-stories-by.tumblr.com** we would love to hear from you.

Don't forget to check out our other promotional channels at:

Websites:
www.FunnyShortStoriesBy.com
www.just-think.com.au

You Tube Channel:
www.youtube.com/JustThinkProperty

Facebook:
www.facebook.com/Just.Think.Group

Linked In: Profile:
http://www.linkedin.com/profile/edit?
trk=hb_tab_pro_top

Linked In: Group:
http://www.linkedin.com/groups/Just-Think-Property-4288955?gid=4288955&trk=hb_side_g

Twitter:
www.twitter.com/justthink1

emails:

edwin@just-think.com.au

sue@just-think.com.au

sue@funnyshortstoriesby.com

Now may we ask a favor from you. We would really appreciate if you would write a review for us on **www.Amazon.com.**

When you do email your details to sue@funnyshortstoriesby.com and we will surprise you with a gift.

About The Authors:

Edwin Almeida:

Edwin's experience is as vast as it is interesting.

The Almeida Family emigrated from Ecuador to Australia when Edwin was seven. Enjoying his childhood years in Australia with his five sisters. His Hot Latin Blood getting him into some scrapes, the "school of hard knocks" taught him to think and act quickly and decisively.

Edwin has packed a lifetime of business experience into his working years with many of these experiences equipping him extremely well for his role of Licensee and owner of Just Think Real Estate.

Starting with a management position in the Building Industry (office and on-site) working in Project Management, Development, Marketing and Sales. An opportunity was offered to then move into Real Estate, which Edwin found to be his passion and has been part of for nine years. With the last five years as a Partner starting two successful, independent Real Estate

Agencies. Each agency incorporating both Sales and Property Management.

Edwin's other interest is Law. This knowledge has proven to be an outstanding and unique benefit to his Real Estate Agency and its clients.

Edwin is actively involved in the local chapters of Chamber of Commerce, Real Estate Institute (REI), BNI (Business Network International) and has articles regularly published in Real Estate Industry related magazines.

To complete this package is Edwin's unique online presence. The benefits to Just Think Real Estate and its client base has been enormous and one that very few Real Estate Professionals could even come close to matching. With more than a hundred videos on Just Think's You Tube Channel, daily activity on a very active nine hundred plus Linked In group plus Facebook and Twitter.

All these links and contacts are all listed in the Introduction and Conclusion sections of this book.

For the assistance and guidance Edwin has given to many people, in particular Landlords

Sue has bestowed upon Edwin the Title

"The Landlords Crusader"

Sue Elliott:

Sue has worked full time in the Real Estate Industry for twelve years enjoying a number of roles. Five years ago becoming a Fully Licensed Agent.

Sue couldn't wait to leave school and start work. At sixteen her first job was a tea girl for a Stock Brokering company in Sydney. Sue soon moved up to share clerk for two large international oil companies, then graduated into International Banking.

A few years on it was time for a change. What does any young, outdoors girl who has been stuck inside for a few years do. A "bread run". A large Bakery was looking for an energetic person with Customer Relations skills to take over a neglected "bread run". They required someone who could grow the customer base and sales volume so they could sell it as a micro business. Sue excelled at this, rejuvenating five neglected "bread runs" which were all sold for a nice profit.

A few years on, time came for a new direction into the Building Industry as Office Manager for an Industrial Roofing Company.

Sue married the son of the business owner, together they expanded into the Maintenance Field and became the main contracting company for two major Petroleum Oil Firms. They remained settled in this field for twenty years.

Having a few investment properties, Sue's next interest was Real Estate. Sue found herself back into Customer Relations for a Property Firm, then onto Sales. She was head hunted by a Property Developer and offered a partnership to start a new Real Estate Agency.

A year later Sue sold her portion of the business and took up a position of Personal Assistant to the same Property Developer.

A few years later Sue was lured back into Real Estate with her previous partner, Edwin Almeida.

Working with Edwin in Just Think Real Estate, they have now lent their hand to Authors and and soon to be Publishers.

Sue is the proud mother of two wonderful boys (now men) and grandmother of three beautiful grandchildren. Some of the family are featured in photos in this book. The last three years Sue has taken on the role of full time carer for her elderly mother.

Photo Resources:

Our thanks to:

stock.xchang   http://sxc.hu

dreamstime   http://www.dreamstime.com

123RF   http://www.123rf.com

Christopher Elliott   my ex model son   for his photo wearing an apron while doing the housework (page 80).

Tahliya Elliott and Lachlan Elliott two of my beautiful grandchildren for them baking and enjoying banana cake and milk (page 91).

Amazon Review:

Reminder – we would appreciate if you could leave a review on our book page.

Don't forget to email Sue and let her know that you left a review, leave your details and we'll forward you a thank you gift for your time. sue@funnyshortstoriesby.com

Regards Edwin and Sue

FunnyShortStoriesBy.com

Made in the USA
Lexington, KY
25 February 2015